A KID'S GUIDE TO THE X Games ™

SKATEBOARDING

in the X Games

CHRISTOPHER BLOMQUIST

The Rosen Publishing Group's

PowerKids Press ™

New York

For two Xtremely wonderful nephews, Timothy and James

Safety gear, including helmets, wrist guards, kneepads, and elbow pads should be worn while skateboarding.
Do not attempt tricks without proper gear, instruction, and supervision.

Published in 2003 by The Rosen Publishing Group, Inc.
29 East 21st Street, New York, NY 10010

First Edition

Editor: Nancy MacDonell Smith
Book Design: Mike Donnellan and Michael de Guzman

Photo Credits: Cover, pp. 11, 12 © Rob Tringali Jr./SportsChrome USA; pp. 4, 7 © Maura B. McConnell; p.8 © Bob Falcetti/Icon SMI; p. 15 © Tomasso DeRosa/SportsChrome USA; p. 16 © Tony Donaldson/SportsChrome USA; p. 19 © Icon Sports Media; p. 21 © Tony Donaldson/Icon SMI.

Blomquist, Christopher.
Skateboarding in the X games / by Christopher Blomquist.— 1st ed.
    p. cm. — (A kid's guide to the X Games)
Includes bibliographical references (p.   ) and index.
  ISBN 0-8239-6300-4 (lib. bdg.)
1. Skateboarding—Juvenile literature. 2. ESPN X-Games—Juvenile literature. [1. Skateboarding. 2. Extreme sports.] I. Title.
  GV859.8 .B56 2003
  796.22–dc21

                                                                      2001006173

Manufactured in the United States of America

Contents

In a trick called an ollie, a skater jumps into the air while keeping his feet on the board. This is a difficult trick to learn.

What Is Skateboarding?

In the sport called skateboarding, a person balances on a four-wheeled board, or **deck**, and coasts along a hard surface. The skater uses his or her feet to make the board roll or stop.

Some skateboarding moves are quite simple to do. One such move is to roll slowly on a flat, open area, such as an empty parking lot. Some tricks are much harder. These tricks include a jump called an **ollie**, and a **kickturn**, which changes the board's direction. These advanced tricks are often done at very fast speeds and on steep or bumpy surfaces. Skaters can easily fall and can hurt themselves while trying these tricks. They wear helmets and pads to protect themselves.

Skateboarding is an **extreme sport**. Extreme sports are also called action sports. No matter what you call them, these sports include a lot of tricks, danger, and action.

Skateboarding and the X Games

The X Games is held in a different U.S. city each summer and winter. The winter X Games has winter sports, such as snowboarding and skiboarding. The summer X Games has summer sports, such as street luge and skateboarding.

X-Games **athletes** try to win prizes and prize money. Gold **medals** are the first-place prizes. Silver medals are the second-place prizes. Bronze medals are the third-place prizes.

Skateboarding has been an X-Games sport ever since the first X Games in 1995. Those games took place in Rhode Island, and 198,000 people attended. Since then X-Games crowds have grown. More than 234,000 people attended the summer 2001 X Games in Philadelphia, Pennsylvania!

More than 234,000 people turned out to see athletes such as Andy Macdonald (left) and Tony Hawk (right) at the 2001 summer X Games in Philadelphia, Pennsylvania.

8

Shaun White tried one of his fanciest tricks on the half-pipe
at the 2001 X Trials in San Diego, California.

Picking Skaters for the X Games

A group called World Cup Skateboarding (WCS) makes the rules for all the skateboarding events at the X Games. One of WCS's tasks is to find the world's best skaters and to invite these athletes to participate in the X Games.

The gold medalists from the previous year's X Games are always invited back. The other skaters **qualify** because they won or did well in **competitions** held throughout the year in the United States, Canada, South America, and Europe.

Two events called the X Trials are held a few months before the X Games. The winners of these **trials** are also invited to the X Games.

Many of the judges for the X Games and the X Trials used to be skaters themselves. Becoming judges is a way for them to stay involved with the sport after they stop competing.

Vert is short for **vertical**. In vert events, athletes skate in a wooden, *U*-shaped **half-pipe**. At the 1999 X Games in San Francisco, California, 31-year-old Tony Hawk made X-Games history during the vert best trick event. After 11 tries, Hawk managed to do two-and-a-half rotations in the air on his board and still land smoothly. Hawk's trick was called a **nine-hundred**. It was the first time any skater did this trick! Hawk won the gold medal. The other skaters lifted him up and carried him in the air as the crowd cheered. Today Hawk still thrills crowds when he does a nine-hundred.

At the 2000 X Games, 27-year-old Bucky Lasek of Maryland won a gold medal in the one-person vert singles event for the second year in a row. Skaters win points by showing how well they can handle their boards.

Bucky Lasek scored 98.5 out of 100 points in the vert singles event at the 2000 X Games. His score is still the highest score ever awarded in vert singles.

Andy Macdonald is one of the top skaters in the world. He and Tony Hawk, another top skater, skate together in the vert doubles event.

Star Skaters at the X Games

Tony Hawk is considered to be the greatest skater of all time. Hawk has skated at every X Games since the first one in 1995. He has won at least one medal every year. Hawk now has a total of 13 medals. This ties him with bicyclist Dave Mirra as the X-Games athlete with the most medals.

Hawk earned five of his gold medals by skating with his good friend Andy Macdonald, of California, in the vert doubles event. In vert doubles, a team of two people skate on the half-pipe at the same time. Hawk and Macdonald have won first place in vert doubles every year since 1997, the first year the event was part of the X Games. Macdonald has skated in every summer X Games in history, too. He has 11 medals, including seven gold medals, three silver medals, and one bronze medal.

The Vert Events

The half-pipe used in the vert events is 12 ½ feet (4 m) high and 56 feet (17 m) wide. There are three vert events in skateboarding. They are vert singles, vert doubles, and vert best trick. Skaters go one at a time in vert singles. The 10 skaters who make the final round do three runs. In vert doubles, the athletes skate in pairs. The five best pairs make it to the finals.

In vert best trick, all the skaters share the half-pipe for one 20-minute period. During that time, each skater tries to show the judges his best trick. In 2000, Bob Burnquist of Brazil won the gold medal for doing a backward move called a **fakie**. Matt Dove of Newport, California, won in 2001 for doing two full spins in the air before landing. The 2001 X Games was the first X Games in which Dove had ever skated!

In the vert doubles event, two skaters are on the half-pipe at the same time. If they're not careful, they could crash into each other!

The park event has the most mixed course of all the X-Games skateboarding events. Skaters have to use quarter-pipes, ramps, stairs, and handrails.

The Park Event

The park event takes place on a specially designed course that includes *J*-shaped **quarter-pipes**, ramps, and even stairs and handrails. Skaters are judged on the difficulty of the tricks that they do. Twenty skaters take two runs. The two runs are rated by six judges. The skaters are supposed to skate through the entire course, which is 160 feet (49 m) by 130 feet (40 m). After each run, a skater's highest and lowest scores are dropped and his remaining four scores are **averaged**. At the end, whoever has the highest average score wins.

Chris Senn of California won the gold medal in the park event in 1995, 1997, and 1999. Brazilian skater Rodil de Araujo Jr. has also won a park event gold medal three times. He won in 1996, 1998, and 2001. Eric Koston of Los Angeles, California, won the park event in 2000.

The Street Events

   The first true X-Games skateboarding street event happened at the 2001 X Games in Philadelphia, Pennsylvania. That year the city of Philadelphia allowed skaters to skate in a public plaza, not a specially built park. This plaza surrounds Philadelphia's City Hall. The plaza's many stairs and ledges are great to skate on, but skating there is against the law. The city made an exception to this rule for the street events at the 2001 X Games.

   Skaters make three 75-second runs in the street event. In 2001, Kerry Getz of Philadelphia won the gold medal, Eric Koston won the silver medal, and Chris Senn of California came in third. Later that day, Rick McCrank of Vancouver, Canada, won the street best trick event. McCrank won for doing a series of flips.

Kerry Getz won the gold medal in the street event at the 2001 X Games. Though Getz isn't wearing a helmet and pads, it's important to wear safety gear every time you skate.

A Talk with Andy Macdonald

How have the X Games changed since 1995?
The general public understands more about skateboarding now than they ever have. They view the sport as a sport. Five years ago it was just like, "Whoa, these guys are crazy."

Do you have a favorite X-Games event that you skate in?
Best trick is right up there because there is no **pressure** to stay on your board . . . . Probably my most favorite, and what I most enjoy, is skating in the doubles.

What has been your favorite X Games?
The summer of '98 X Games. I was the most relaxed I have ever been for a competition . . . I ended up skating the best that I have skated.

How do you prepare for a vert run?
   The **routine** that you're going to do you've already skated in

Andy Macdonald ▶

practice, and you know what you're doing when you drop in [to the pipe].

What do you think is ahead for skateboarding?
I can only see it growing and getting bigger and becoming more and more popular.

Do you have any advice for kids who want be X-Games skateboarding champs one day?
Just start skating because you love it . . . . You've got to love skateboarding and want to do it all the time just because you love to do it, not because you want to be **sponsored** or be in the X Games some day.

A Look Ahead

Athletes will skate in vert, park, and the newest event, street, at future summer X Games. For the 2002 summer X Games, the organizers worked to get better seating at Philadelphia's City Hall plaza for the street skateboarding events. Most of the crowd had to stand in 2001, so not everyone could see the action clearly.

As skateboarding's popularity continues to grow with young people, younger athletes will learn new tricks and will show off their skills at the X Games. These athletes will become skateboarding's newest stars. They will be the Tony Hawks, the Andy Macdonalds, and the Bob Burnquists of tomorrow.

Glossary

athletes (ATH-leets) People who take part in sports.

averaged (A-vrijd) An athlete's total points divided by the number of scores.

competitions (kom-peh-TIH-shunz) Sports contests.

deck (DEK) The flat, usually wooden part of a skateboard that a skater stands on.

extreme sport (ek-STREEM SPORT) A sport such as bicycle stunt riding, skateboarding, motocross, wakeboarding, street luge, and in-line skating.

fakie (FAY-kee) A trick in which the skateboard moves backwards as the skater stands in a normal position.

half-pipe (HAF-pyp) A ramp that is shaped like a big *U*.

kickturn (KIK-tern) A trick in which the skater puts weight on the back of the skateboard, which lifts the front, and turns the board in another direction.

medals (MEH-dulz) Small, round pieces of metal that are given as awards.

nine-hundred (NYN HUN-dred) A trick in which the skater does two and one-half spins in the air before landing.

ollie (AH-lee) A jump done by tapping the tail of the skateboard on the ground.

pressure (PREH-shur) A push, demand, or requirement.

qualify (KWAH-lih-fy) To meet the requirements of something.

quarter-pipes (KWOR-ter PYPS) Ramps that looks like the halves of half-pipes.

routine (roo-TEEN) The series of tricks an athlete does during a run.

sponsored (SPAHN-serd) To be paid by a company.

trials (TRYLZ) Sports events held before the X Games to test and find new athletes.

vertical (VUR-tih-kul) In an up-and-down direction.

Index

Web Sites

Due to the changing nature of internet links, PowerKids Press has developed an online list of Web sites related to the subject of this book. This site is updated regularly. Please use this link to access the list.

www.powerkidslinks.com/kgxg/skatinx